J. G. Milne works late on a spring afternoon, preparing fields to plant corn on his Eaton farm.

Colorado's Centennial Farms & Ranches
A Century of Seasons

Photography and Text by Michael Lewis
with Joanne Ditmer

WESTCLIFFE PUBLISHERS, INC., ENGLEWOOD, COLORADO

ACKNOWLEDGEMENTS

For my wife, Sharon, who makes my life richer,
and for my parents, who always believed.

As with any project of this type, there are many people to thank. Ann Moscicki with Eastman Kodak's Professional Imaging Division gave me a big boost in the early months of this project by contributing all of the film. In 1992 when personal finances prevented me from spending as much time on the project as I needed, two organizations came to my aid. Skip Kohloff, President of the Colorado Photographic Arts Center, was instrumental in offering that group's sponsorship. This, in turn, made it possible for the US West Foundation to award me a grant, enabling me to complete a large amount of work. I appreciate the efforts of Jane Prancan, Director of the US West Foundation.

Many of my colleagues offered input and help along the way. Emmett Jordan, Dave Denney, Paul Keebler, and Joel Grimes were invaluable, and their contributions can never be repaid with mere words.

I would also like to thank Rich Clarkson, Steve Lang, Janet Reeves, Steve Larson, Paul Curtis, Tom Kennedy, Tom Brock, Chuck and Petra Bigger, Dave Turner, Nan Glick, Meg Van Ness, Lane Ittleson, the fine staff at the Denver Public Library's Western History section, and Erica Berger, who told me to get closer to my subjects.

My thanks to the talented people at Westcliffe Publishers, especially John Fielder, Suzanne Venino, Leslie Gerarden, and Dianne Howie, who shared my vision for *Centennial Farms & Ranches*. The contributions of Joanne Ditmer, Patricia Limerick, and Sharyn Yeoman gave this book a valuable historical perspective. And finally, to the farmers and ranchers and their families who treated me like a member of the family, tolerated my questions, and never gave me a bad horse — my heartfelt thanks.

International Standard Book Number: 1-56579-050-2

Library of Congress Catalog Number: 94-060591

Copyright © Michael Lewis, 1994. All rights reserved.

Published by Westcliffe Publishers, 2650 South Zuni Street, Englewood, Colorado 80110

Publisher, John Fielder; Editor, Suzanne Venino; Designer, Leslie Gerarden; Proofreader, Bonnie Beach

First frontispiece: Joe Gallegos walks through a field of black-eyed Susans on his San Luis ranch while searching for saplings he planted as a windbreak.

Title page: Tom Eppich takes a break from cutting oats on the ranch that his great-grandfather started in 1887 near Mancos.

Steam rises from the backs of Belgian draft horses pulling a hay sled on the Cottonwood Ranch near Granby.

Joe Gallegos and his father, Corpus, watch the sun set over bean fields they have been irrigating.

PREFACE

I've always liked farmers. Maybe it's because my great-grandfather farmed and it's still in my blood. Or maybe it's because I grew up in rural Missouri and most of my friends and classmates lived on farms. Their fathers were hard-working men with a sense of humor and a sense of purpose. After working in the hayfields during the summers of my high school years, I understood why some of my buddies didn't follow in their father's footsteps. Coaxing a living from the land is damn hard work. And sometimes hard work isn't enough to overcome the forces of nature. It wasn't that the sons weren't as tough as their fathers, it's just that something else, something stronger, pulled them from the land. I am in awe of families who have dedicated generations of work to the land. Especially the same land.

My family no longer farms. I didn't even follow in my father's footsteps. I chose to be a photojournalist. As a photographer, I've always wanted to do a long-term project that would allow me to know a subject intimately. In the world of daily journalism, spending a day or even two on a story is a rare luxury. And as a freelance photographer, time is ruled by the need to earn a living. The thought of spending enough time on one subject to produce a book was only a dream.

In August 1990, I attended a photography workshop in Steamboat Springs, organized and staffed by photographers with ties to *National Geographic* magazine. The head of the workshop, Rich Clarkson, a former director of photography at the Geographic, advised me to look close to home for a project and not to rely on an exotic location for the strength of my work. Driving back from the workshop along the Colorado River near Hot Sulphur Springs, I watched a rancher cutting hay. I had my topic: centennial farms and ranches.

I had first learned about Colorado's centennial farms and ranches from stories in *The Denver Post* written by Joanne Ditmer. The program was started in 1986 by the Colorado Historical Society, the Colorado State Fair, and the State Department of Agriculture to honor the families whose farm or ranch had been in the same family for a hundred years or more. I obtained the names of about 120 families from the historical society and mailed out questionnaires. I received almost 90 completed questionnaires, then visited more than 35 families to see who I could include in the project. My criteria was simple: the people and the land had to be interesting. Also, I wanted to have a good cross-section of farms and ranches both by location and size. I eventually narrowed the list down to eight, and in the next few years I visited these families during each of the seasons. Usually, I was a guest in their homes and would stay for several days. In most cases, I would shoot during the early morning and evening hours to take advantage of the soft light. When the light was harsh during the middle of the day, I offered my help with chores and it was usually accepted.

It was a little daunting when I climbed onto a horse for the first time in 30 years, but I tried to watch and learn and hoped that I wouldn't make a fool of myself. Since I hadn't oversold my horsemanship, the ranchers didn't have very high expectations. Yet it was hard to contain a grin when Larry Ward critiqued my cowboying after eight hours of herding cows: "I thought we'd be able to give you a lot of ribbing after today, but you did alright."

I've tried to show some of the work that puts the food on our tables and to tell the stories of the people who are descended from the pioneers that settled Colorado. In a time when everyone seems to be from some-where else, it's no small accomplishment to have worked the same land for a hundred or more years. I hope, through this book, that you get to know these people as I've had the pleasure to know them.

— Michael Lewis
Denver, Colorado

A HISTORICAL PERSPECTIVE

by Patricia Nelson Limerick and Sharyn Yeoman

Changing Times for Colorado Farmers and Ranchers

A plane takes off in Denver and the suburban sprawl below finally clears away. Passengers in window seats look down at the plains of Colorado. "Good heavens," they say, "there's nothing down there."

Nothing? Nothing but years of labor, years of human life, invested in the land. Just below the illusion of emptiness lies the agrarian history of Colorado, a mosaic composed of heroism and frustration, achievement and error, success and failure.

Working against stiff odds, the farmers and ranchers portrayed in the following photographs and essays have kept the farm in the family — and the family on the farm — for one hundred years or more. The state of Colorado recognizes this achievement with the designation of "Centennial Farm" or "Centennial Ranch." To date, there are 188 centennial farms and ranches listed by the Colorado Historical Society.

The first farmers here migrated north along river basins from New Mexico around 500 A.D. Anasazi Indians at Mesa Verde grew hardy crops of maize, beans, and squash — foods that could be dried and stored, enabling these first settlers to build permanent villages. By 1100 A.D. construction of dwellings built into the steep-sided walls of mesas concentrated these people into large towns. Trying to support a growing population, the Anasazi made increased use of poorer soils; combined with drought, this turn to less productive farming probably led to abandonment of the cliff dwellings after only two centuries.

On the other side of the Rocky Mountains, in the Great Basin, people of the desert culture — the Washo, Shoshoni, Paiute, and Ute — practiced simple agriculture. Burning off grasslands in the fall and sowing surplus seed brought greater yields of edible grass seed in the spring. They diverted streams, creating meadows and producing a year-round food supply, surviving for hundreds of years in an area deemed uninhabitable by whites.

Spanish colonization introduced a new set of practices. Along the Huerfano, Cucharas, and Purgatoire rivers, citizens of northern Mexico irrigated small farms. Settlers arrived in Colorado's San Luis Valley when

Mexico approved extensive land grants between 1837 and 1846 to encourage settlement as a barrier against raiding Indians and land-hungry Americans. These settlers were experienced farmers, with the knowledge, supplies, and livestock to farm and to feed themselves.

The United States promised to respect land titles in the areas ceded by the Treaty of Guadalupe Hidalgo at the close of the Mexican-American War. While Spanish-speaking people made their way north, the fur trade brought Anglo-Americans to the Colorado plains. The exchange of skins and furs for manufactured goods and agricultural produce at trading posts, such as Bent's Fort on the Arkansas River, stimulated the growth of agriculture. These small outposts provided a refuge for explorers and adventurers like John C. Fremont, who prepared reports, maps, and descriptions that inspired the imaginations of settlers.

Mining booms brought a sudden energy and interest in Colorado agricultural development. During the winter of 1859, demand for food exceeded supply, as hopeful miners rushed into the Pike's Peak region seeking gold. Even in the midst of the wildest mining frenzy, some new Coloradans saw a greater stability in agricultural enterprise. William N. Byers, founding editor and owner of Colorado's first newspaper, the *Rocky Mountain News*, declared in the first issue:

"From present appearances our citizens are likely to all be taken off with the Cherry Creek yellow fever in as much that the farming interests of our territory are likely to suffer materially and miners will also have to suffer for want of supplies. This is all wrong; and our opinion is that farmers who stay at home and spend as much money to improve and cultivate their

Opposite: Years of farm equipment sit idle on the Godsey Family Farm near Wray.

farms will realize more clear profit by so doing than they will to go to the mines."

Byers promoted agricultural opportunity in Colorado to attract permanent settlers. In his conviction that the most desirable settlers were farmers, Byers reinforced a well-established American belief that farmers provided the foundation for democratic government based in land ownership. This agrarian ideal offered a vision of a hardy, self-sufficient society based on the independence and sound morality of small landholders. Farmers, the theory went, fostered industriousness, frugality, and self-sufficiency, while the circumstances of urban industrial workers denied them the healthful effects of the land and the independent security of self-sufficiency.

In the 1870s, with the sometimes bloody and brutal process of Indian removal close to completion, Colorado's abundance of land stood in contrast with its sparse settlement. Publicity generated by the Union Colony, a communal farming enterprise reported in the *New York Tribune*, created interest in Colorado as a destination for farmers. As farms sprang up along rivers, water alloca-  tion became a concern. People who invested in the labor and money to build reservoirs and ditches demanded protection against the threat of upstream appropriations. In 1879 state water rights legislation, granting the first user the greatest claim to water, formed the basis for a system of water allocation which other western states later emulated. Land within easy reach of irrigation water filled with farms by 1880, and the crowded river valleys discouraged new migrants.

Federal policy also played a significant role in settlement. With the Homestead Act of 1862, settlers could claim 160 acres of farmland and gain title by paying a small fee, making improvements, and farming for five years. After six months, a homesteader could pay $1.25 per acre to receive title early. Many landless farmers used this homesteading opportunity to acquire land of their own, building permanent homes as soon as their economic situation permitted. In the semi-arid West, however, 160 acres was an awkward size, for irrigated farms required much less land and ranches much more.

Despite an influx of homesteaders, Colorado had an image problem. The reports of explorers like Zebulon Pike and Stephen H. Long pictured all western plains as the "Great American Desert." Settlers avoided the Colorado plains until innovators figured out methods of dryland farming and improved transportation to urban markets.

In 1870, the newly constructed Denver Pacific Railroad, running between Denver and Cheyenne, connected the plains of Colorado to the national transportation network, linking Colorado farmers with urban markets. A few months later the Kansas Pacific arrived, connecting Denver to Kansas City and points east. Rapid expansion of railroad lines in Colorado stimulated a rate of population growth along the Front Range which seemed incredible to long-term residents. Railroad promoters sold land in Colorado and publicized the whole region.

The years 1887 and 1888, the peak of homestead claim entry in Colorado, coincided with the extension of the railroad into eastern Colorado and with a relatively wet period in the climactic cycle. Believing that "rain follows the plow," migrants streamed through Kansas into Colorado's "rain belt." While these farmers competed with Colorado's existing farmers for markets, they were also consumers of goods and services, causing small towns to spring up along railroad lines.

Most farm families were self-sufficient, and their surplus provided food for rapidly expanding urban populations. Industry relied on farm-produced raw materials, and buying patterns encouraged specialization on the farm. Colorado-produced livestock, wool, and wheat stimulated growth in meat packing, textile, and milling factories. Farming profits permitted farmers to buy new machines to cultivate and harvest their crops. In the early 1880s, abundant rainfall, booster publicity, the growth of local economies, and improved transportation combined to draw people to the area. Over-ambitious expectations and the lack of knowledge about arid

climates, however, created a pattern of corn crops ill-suited to the Colorado plains.

The agricultural boom on the plains literally dried-up with a drought cycle beginning in 1889. The year 1894, the driest on record, coincided with a return of ravenous grasshoppers. These natural disasters, accompanied by falling farm prices, left many farmers stranded and destitute on failing claims. Speculation in western mortgages had attracted eastern investors; now, with starkly diminished profits, capital investment from outside the region abruptly ended. Towns shrank or even disappeared, and railroad lines stood unused as production fell and farmers left the land. Farmers learned a hard lesson: rain, it turned out, did not follow the plow.

Cattlemen, like farmers, suffered severe losses in the 1890s. Spring and summer drought, followed by severe winter weather, depleted herds. Some of the farmers who held on recognized the opportunity presented by the cattlemen's hard times and started growing fodder for winter feed. Cattlemen themselves began farming to supplement feed. Wheat acreage displaced corn. In fact, wheat production actually expanded during these difficult times, with new varieties of seed adapted to aridity, winter cold, and local soil conditions. Irrigation became a necessity for agricultural survival on the Colorado plains.

Irrigation systems, on the scale necessary to carry water to thousands of acres of dry land, cost more than individual farmers could afford. In their search for capital, farmers turned to the federal government. The first federal effort in Colorado, the Uncompahgre Reclamation Project, was a twelve-mile tunnel through the Rocky Mountains, carrying water from the Gunnison River to the Uncompahgre Valley. Marked by controversies over who should bear the cost of construction, the project delivered its first water in 1908. The government intended to advance the necessary funds, increase the number of irrigated farms, and then rebalance the account with payments from the farmers, but projects like the Gunnison Tunnel never reached this moment of balance. Farmers needed larger units than 160 acres to repay the debt from massive irrigation projects. Eventually the cost of water from irrigation forced some families from the land. Farm sizes increased as failed farmers sold

out to neighbors who needed more land to generate the income to pay increased irrigation costs.

The hard times of the 1890s spread discontent into the political arena. As difficult as drought and pests had been, farmers felt that the forces of industrialization and the concentration of capital posed even greater hardships. As industries consolidated into corporations that handled all the processes involved in finishing farm products, farmers occupied an increasingly risky position in the market. A meat processor bought cattle, fattened them at feed lots, butchered, packaged, transported and sold meat as their own brand. Buyers for large companies required farmers to specialize, and farms that once produced enough variety for self-sufficiency now produced one commodity.

Profound changes in transportation, banking, and mechanization made farmers more and more dependent. Large corporate monopolies, farmers complained, controlled the cost of transportation, the prices of farm commodities, and access to loans for expansion or modernization. With efforts at cooperative marketing and purchasing, institutions like the Grange gave farmers at least limited control over some aspects of their lives. The People's Party, or Populism, attempted to counter the influence of industrial capital with political power. Populists argued that the growing power of business in transportation, industry, and finance denied farmers a fair return for their labor and investment. In Colorado, the People's Party became a powerful third party. In a bid to expand their political power, the Populists combined with Democrats in the elections of 1896. Republican William McKinley's defeat of William Jennings Bryan, joint candidate of the Populists and the Democrats, was virtually the end of this third party. For the first time, American economic and

political power lay outside agriculture; industrial interests now carried the day.

After the agrarian failures and defeats of the 1890s, the new century seemed to offer revived hope. Farm prices and land values rose sharply across the nation, nearly doubling in the first decade of the twentieth century. Agricultural expansion slowed, easing competition; with more  people now working in industry and living in cities, markets for farm products grew. Farmers began to work all but the most marginal farmlands. Production stabilized as increasing demand from urban industrial centers, such as Denver, St. Louis, and Chicago, absorbed surpluses. Foreign demand skyrocketed when the onset of World War I crippled European agriculture.

The period from 1900 to 1920 was the golden age of Colorado agriculture. The prices that farmers received for their products rose in relationship to non-farm commodities. Ranchers reclaimed marginal farmlands for grazing; thousands of cattle grazed behind barbed wire on cultivated grasses. Sugar beets and the manufacture of sugar became Colorado's single greatest cash crop, and the byproducts from the processing of sugar beets fattened cattle in feedlots. A significant amount of Colorado's land remained in the public domain, and, in a common pattern, sheep and cattle ranchers grazed their livestock on lands leased from the government while they grew feed on their own property.

The Great Depression may have begun in 1929 for the rest of the nation, but in rural Colorado it began years earlier. Farm income declined disastrously in 1921 and purchasing power fell to 67% of its pre-1920 level. Declining world markets and increasing competition from livestock-producing nations like Australia reduced farm incomes even more. Many farmers found themselves stretching much smaller incomes while trying to pay back the loans they had acquired to expand during the good years. Farmers and ranchers struggled to force the federal government to regulate price-depressing surpluses and to help them find some relief from their debts. Operating expenses, meanwhile, did not fall as far or as fast as farm commodity prices, which forced many farmers to raise production levels; but increasing surpluses caused prices to fall still further.

Farm foreclosures rose, and urban industrial areas absorbed the rural refugees. Groups like the Grange, the Farmers Alliance, and the Farmers Union demanded federal intervention and farm relief. Responding to the pleas of farmers, Congress offered the Agricultural Adjustment Act of 1933, attempting to restore parity (the ratio of earnings to costs) by paying cash rewards for limiting production of certain farm commodities plagued by continued surpluses.

As the economic downturn of the 1920s and 1930s worsened, small farmers and tenant farmers quit farming, while large farmers tried to increase production by plowing more land. Overgrazing and mechanized tilling of marginal land loosened soil usually held in place by natural grasses, and drought years beginning in 1931 brought dust storms that darkened the skies. The Soil Conservation Service, formed by Franklin Roosevelt as part of the New Deal, gave farmers advice about windbreaks and contour plowing, but no one offered a strategy to reduce the market pressure that caused farmers to put marginal land into production. Most of the land had recovered by 1940, but increased wheat prices during World War II sparked a repeat bout of expanded production, in turn causing another near dust bowl in the 1950s, with another near miss in the 1970s. As farmers left the land, corporations and absentee farmers, often called suitcase farmers, bought up the available acreage. More and more, low profit margins per acre eliminated all but the largest landowners, as only large-scale operations could thrive.

Three major technological developments in the twentieth century fostered an agricultural revolution throughout the United States: the internal combustion engine, rural electrification, and the increasing appli-

cation of science to agriculture. By 1950, the internal combustion engine completely replaced horses as the mobile source of farm power. Tractors enabled farmers to plant more land than ever before and in less time. Maintenance took less time and effort than keeping horses. Money saved on labor bought more land, now necessary to maximize the investment in tractor technology. Access to capital to purchase tractors and mechanized equipment gave some farmers competitive advantages over their neighbors, leading to further concentration of land in fewer hands and moving farming still closer to agribusiness.

Electricity reached most farms by 1960, ending rural isolation and powering farm machinery. Mechanical milking machines replaced human labor in dairy operations while automated feed dispensers fed livestock. Turbine pumps and moveable sprinklers brought more land into production, watering fields of wheat, corn, beets, and alfalfa. By 1970, however, the water table supporting most of plains farming had dropped thirty-six feet, and it continues to drop precipitously.

The application of science increased efficiency as pesticides, herbicides, fertilizers, and applied genetics decreased labor and increased productivity. Technology displaced farm workers and rural communities dwindled. Many institutions — churches, fraternal orders, and farm groups — closed as populations declined. The high cost of technology prohibited young farmers from starting out on their own; in the 1980s the investment to begin farming exceeded $250,000 for technology alone. These high costs favored large agribusiness over small diversified family farms, and investments in technology also reduced choice; farmers with large debts to pay could not afford to stop pumping or using chemicals.

In the 1980s many family farmers reaped the unhappy consequences of expansion during the 1960s and 1970s, struggling with debts they had undertaken with optimism just a few years before. Newspapers and television showed images of families huddled together as the parts and pieces of their lives moved across the auction block. "I'll take responsibility for expanding too fast in the 1970s," one man said, explaining his family's loss of their century-old farm. "But the banks were too willing to extend credit and the farmers too willing to take it."

In 1986, experts estimated that nearly 40% of Colorado farmers were on the edge of bankruptcy.

Many of the farmers who were able to hold on to their farms now find themselves in competition with real estate developers, expanding urban populations, and recreational industries. Ski condos sprawl across haying meadows; rafters vie for control of river flows; and governments of growing urban areas jealously eye agriculture's water supply.

In that competition, today's centennial farmers and ranchers face problems their great-grandparents never imagined. In too many cases, the modern agricultural economy asks farmers to take all of the risks in return for uncertain benefits and rewards. Often taking outside jobs to keep the family farm financially viable, these people put into practice most of the virtues associated with the pioneers of a vanished frontier West: a strong work ethic, determination, persistence, frugality, fierce family loyalty, and deep affection for nature and the land. In the current campaign to preserve and respect the West's natural beauty, we surely have an equal obligation to preserve and respect the best of the West's human heritage.

Patricia Nelson Limerick is a professor of history at the University of Colorado in Boulder and the author of *A Legacy of Conquest: The Unbroken Past of the American West*. Sharyn Yeoman is a graduate student at CU Boulder and the Colorado coordinator of National History Day.

Charles Plumb, 94, beneath a photograph of his grandmother, who homesteaded the White-Plumb Farm west of Greeley.

S P R I N G

Milne Farm — Weld County

The rhythms of the land dictate the lives of its human inhabitants even as we near the twenty-first century. Seamless seasons, an endless cycle of plowing, sowing, harvesting...calving and lambing, branding and shearing, shipping to market...surviving droughts and blizzards, the joy of spring turning the countryside a luminous new green once again.

That unceasing, compelling rhythm is a way of life for generations of Coloradans who have worked the same land for a century or more. Their livelihood pivots on the weather, and, despite its unpredictability, most farmers and ranchers can imagine no other way of life. Yet, for farm families who need to get their crops in the ground and ranchers who have baby calves and lambs to tend, the mercurial behavior of the weather can be devastating.

An old Colorado adage states: If you don't like the weather, wait fifteen minutes and it will change. That's particularly true in the spring, when balmy breezes and sunshiny days can tempt one into believing warm weather is on the way, only to be slammed by a bitter snowstorm.

Fortunately, such fickleness rarely matches the weather that came in the winter of 1949, called the year of the great blizzards. *The Denver Post* reported that from the beginning of January snowstorms raged for some 25 days that winter. In the first month and a half of the new year, temperatures dropped as low as minus fifty degrees, winds blew 80 miles per hour, and more than a hundred people died across the Rocky Mountains and the Great Plains.

Sunday, January 2, was a deceptive day. With temperatures predicted to reach a pleasant forty to fifty degrees, the Jim Milne, Jr., family, buoyed by a church service and a bountiful dinner, decided to stroll around the family farm. Within an hour the temperature dropped ten degrees. The cutting wind blew snow at their backs as they hurried home to the warmth of the wood-burning stove. A blinding blizzard howled for days, stranding livestock in the fields.

"Once the snow started, it blew and blew and blew," recalled J. G. Milne, III, known as Grant. "We had always fed sheep, but, fortunately, we didn't have any that year, else we'd have lost mega dollars.

"Cattle just put their backs to the wind. We'd fed them that Sunday morning, then couldn't get to them until Wednesday. Their eyes froze shut, but once it started to warm up, the icicles fell off and they could see again."

Grant's grandmother had been visiting that Sunday afternoon, planning to return to her house in town that evening, but with the roads closed, she stayed for three days. "I had to dig through fifty-foot-long drifts blocking our access to Highway 85. It was nearly impossible to see and I got frostbite from the wind chill. It took all day to go a half mile," said Grant. "We've had blizzards since, but nothing like that. And I hope I don't see another."

Grant's grandfather, James Grant Milne, left Kirriemuir, Scotland, in 1880 for the New World and a new life. The family had been tenant farmers on the same land for over a hundred years, but James, one of nine boys, wanted to be a landowner. In Weld County, Colorado, he worked for David Boyd, an early pioneer and large landowner. When James heard that there was good land in Idaho available for homesteading, he headed further west. But the land in Idaho struck him as no better than the land in Colorado, and he returned to Weld County in 1888. Boyd put him in touch with a homesteader who wanted to sell his 160 acres. The quarter section had only the original sod dugout for a house, but there was a sturdy barn.

Opposite: J. G. Milne and his family take a break after plotting plow lines on their farm near Eaton. "I hate to see a field that isn't plowed straight."

Five miles north of present-day Greeley, the Milne homestead sits on the plains near the South Platte River. Plenty of feed (alfalfa and beet tops) was grown locally, and the location was close to ranchers bringing their sheep off summer pasture in the mountains and foothills to the west. It seemed to James a good spot for a sheep feeding operation. One of the earliest sheep feeders in the area, James would fatten the animals in a feedlot during the winter months and sell them in the spring. Sheep were essential to the pioneer life, for wool was needed for everything from clothing to the canvas tops of covered wagons.

When James died, his son, Jim, took over. Uneasiness over the unpredictability of Colorado weather led Jim to do something in the 1930s that shocked his neighbors: he dug a well. Other ranchers considered that brash and somewhat foolish, but within a few years they had done the same — as insurance against their ditches running dry.

During the Dust Bowl years of the 1930s, searing drought and blinding dust storms left indelible memories. Farmers watched in horror as never-ceasing winds swept up the powder-dry top soil and scoured the earth into barren dust bowls.

"It was terrible," recalled Jim's wife, Mildred. "In the middle of the day it would be dark from the dust in the air. You didn't go out unless you had to, but we had to...to feed the livestock. You tied wet rags around your face and did it."

Mildred still lives on the ranch, in the old house built in 1892, though there have been some additions. "We've done everything to it," said Grant. "In 1934 Dad raised the roof and put a second floor under it. He built on porches, then glassed them in. In 1946 he had all the dirt dug out from underneath and built a full basement. I always accused him of being a frustrated contractor."

In 1947 Grant's father expanded and diversified his business by starting the Flatirons Company, a sand, gravel, and cement business. He continued feeding sheep and grew potatoes, alfalfa, and sugar beets. When Grant returned from the service in 1960, he went into partnership with his father, managing the farm.

The late 1970s brought big changes to the Milne family's way of life. Because of mounting competition from large corporate feedlots, they decided to close down their sheep feeding operation. They also sold off the cattle, leveled all the fields, and added pumping stations to increase the efficiency of the irrigation ditches. Now J. G. Milne, IV — Jay — does most of the farming, with his brother, Warren, and father helping out during planting and harvesting. Today the Milne family grows corn, beans, alfalfa, and pickle cucumbers; the only livestock on the farm are a few horses and bottle calves — 4H projects for the kids.

Spring no longer means shearing and loading sheep for market. Now Jay spends most of his days on a tractor. The soil has to be prepared for planting — spreading manure, disking, plowing, and bedding. Then, in late spring, as the beans push tender green shoots above the ground, he keeps an uneasy eye on the sky and an ear to the radio for weather reports. More than once a fast-moving hail storm has decimated a young crop. When that happens, all a farmer can do is plant again and hope for better luck. For some, farming as a livelihood is too much of a gamble. For the Milne family, it's a way of life.

J. G. Milne inspects hail-damaged seedlings. The bean sprouts
were so badly damaged that the fields had to be replowed and replanted.

Unloading hay to feed sheep on the Hotchkiss Ranch.

Hotchkiss Ranch — Delta County

The West was settled by young men with wanderlust. Enos T. Hotchkiss was one such young man. Born in Pennsylvania in 1832, from a Scotch-Irish family that came to America in 1642, Enos was twenty-seven years old when he came west to seek his fortune. He worked mines in California, Nevada, Idaho, and Utah before arriving in Colorado in 1874 and setting up camp in what is now Lake City. His years of mining experience paid off when he struck a vein and discovered the Golden Fleece Mine.

Enos befriended and became partners with Otto Mears, known as "the pathfinder of the San Juans," and together they built several toll roads, including one from Denver through Fairplay and on to Saguache and Lake City. Roads were essential to the economic development and settlement of the frontier. As more settlers arrived in Colorado, however, it became clear that the Utes, like Native Americans elsewhere, weren't destined to stay on the land they called home.

In 1879, while living near Powderhorn, a small settlement on the Cebolla River south of Gunnison, Enos heard from the Indian agents at Fort Crawford that the Utes would soon be removed from the country north of the Black Canyon, opening the area to white settlement. Enos, wanting to find the best land, set out to explore it.

Leaving in early August, he traveled alone, following what is now the Blue Mesa Road, then headed north through Montrose. He took a young colt in addition to the mare he was riding, figuring that any Utes who saw his tracks would assume they were stray horses. He continued along the Gunnison and forded the river near present-day Austin. Crossing a high mesa, known today as Rogers Mesa, he rode through rolling fields of white sage as far as he could see. In mid-August, from the crest of a hill, Enos looked down onto the North Fork Valley. Through his spy glass he saw Indian camps at Quackenbush Creek and the site of present-day Paonia. That night he made camp in a clearing in the brush. Eventually, he would build a house at this spot, where the town that bears his name would one day grow.

In 1881, word was spread by the soldiers at Fort Crawford that the Utes would be relocated the following summer. That spring Enos returned to the beautiful valley he had seen two years earlier. Enos, Dave Platt, and brothers George and William Duke left Powderhorn with two wagons loaded with supplies and pulled by teams of oxen. It took them ten days to cross Blue Mesa, and they came down it with huge spruce trees tied behind the wagons to slow their descent.

Meeting a party of miners that the Utes had driven out, Enos assured his group that there was nothing to fear. "We boys wanted to turn back, but Hotchkiss said there was no danger," said George Duke later. The men arrived at the North Fork of the Gunnison, but could not cross it due to the high waters of spring flooding. They built a cabin and, leaving Platt to guard it, went back to Powderhorn for another load. When they returned with additional supplies and some two dozen other men, they found that Platt had gone crazy, killed the dogs, and buried them in the dirt floor of the cabin.

Enos built an adobe house across the river from the original cabin. It was here that he and his second wife, Elizabeth, raised their six children. Enos had married his first wife, Hannah, age 11, in Pennsylvania, and they had three children before divorcing. The oldest, Andrew, traveled with his father and helped with many mining trips and ventures.

By 1882 many other families and settlers had come into the North Fork Valley. Enos was the first to bring in a herd of cattle — 1,500 head. Through the years, homesteaders grazed their cattle on pasture that stretched from Blue Mesa to Marble. Each fall a huge roundup was one of the valley's biggest events, a time for socializing as well as working together.

But that neighborly spirit suffered in 1889 when Enos brought in the first flock of sheep, a payoff from a gambling debt. The sheep grazed in the valley and surrounding mountains as did his cattle, and that infuriated local cattlemen, who charged that the sheep destroyed the grass. Neighbors turned against Enos and started raiding his cattle. Enos hired gunslinger Sam Angeline, who shot two local hands caught stealing Hotchkiss cattle. That stopped the conflict before it became a war.

Today's threat to sheep ranchers is the price of sheep and wool. Wool growers face an uncertain market and an even more uncertain future. "The future is pretty bleak right now, with talk of grazing fees increasing and wool incentives being taken away," said John Hotchkiss, grandson of Enos. He runs the ranch with his nephew, Brian (Kip) Farmer.

"Wool brought about 50 cents a pound in 1993 and that's a break-even price," he continued. "I kept the wool stored from March to October that year, hoping for better prices, but I didn't get them. Some growers are still hanging on to their wool.

"I retire in two years, and then Kip takes over. He'll have to make the decision what to do, maybe cut down on sheep and increase the size of the cattle herd."

The Hotchkiss Ranch runs more than 4,000 ewes, considered a large herd by Colorado standards. (While small numbers of sheep are usually thought of as a flock, western ranchers use the term herd, same as their beef cattle.) Of the nation's sheep producers, 75 percent have less than 50 sheep, according to Tom Kourlis, Colorado Commissioner of Agriculture, who runs a family sheep ranch founded in 1926. Conversely, 25 percent of the producers provide 80 percent of the country's wool and meat.

With that many sheep, chores on the Hotchkiss Ranch tend to take on grand proportions, whether it's lambing, shearing, or moving sheep to summer pasture. In springtime — a cycle of life and birth and new beginnings on a sheep ranch — as many as 400 lambs are born each day during the height of lambing season.

On a cold April morning, Kip arrives at the lambing pens to a cacophony of bleating lambs and ewes, ear-shattering to city folk, but welcome music to sheep ranchers. After the ewes give birth, the day-old lambs are numbered, inoculated, have their tails bobbed, and the males castrated. Everyone — herders and owners — works a 12-hour shift. Longer, if needed.

Two herders work all night, putting each ewe and her lamb (often twins and sometimes triplets) in a pen, making sure each newborn is cared for by its mother. With factory-like precision, mothers and offspring are moved through a series of pens, determined by the age of the lambs, before being put out on spring pasture.

In late May, the sheep are moved to the high country for summer pasture, where they'll stay until September. During that time, fences are mended and hay fields irrigated. Later the hay will be cut, baled, and stacked. In late September, the "fats" are sent to the slaughterhouse, others are shipped to feedlots to be fattened, and in November the rams go into the herd to breed. In April the sheep will be sheared. And then it's lambing time again.

It takes large numbers to make a profit. One of the things that helps keep the ranch going is leasing deeded land to hunting outfitters during elk season. Sheep ranching is a tough way to make a living, but the Hotchkiss family has been doing it for more than 100 years and hopes to be here for many more.

John Hotchkiss likes to tell a joke about the sheep rancher who won the lottery. When asked what he intended to do with the money, the rancher replied, "Oh, I guess I'll keep running sheep until it's all gone."

They haven't won the lottery, but the Hotchkiss family still plans on running sheep.

Just two days old, these newborn lambs have been numbered, their tails docked,
and the males castrated on the Hotchkiss Ranch in Delta County.

On a cold day in March, Don Godsey tags a newborn calf and then pushes it toward its mother.

As day breaks on the Hotchkiss Ranch, Brian Farmer carries a day-old lamb through the lambing shed.

Kirk Schepler walks atop a loaded wagon on the Yount-Schepler Farm near Vernon.

Tom Eppich moves new calves to a shed during a late spring snow.

Gary Schafer, with the help of his neighbors, brands cattle on his ranch near Boyero.

"We burned railroad ties for heat and cooking," remembered Erma Schafer. "Some neighbors burned dried cow chips for fuel." The Great Depression of the 1930s was a memorable era for the Coloradans whose families have worked the same land for more than a century. They survived, and that was a major accomplishment when thousands of farmers and ranchers were forced off their land. The Schafers managed to hang on to the family ranch, which was started in 1873, but times were difficult. "We didn't go to town much, didn't have the money," said Erma, "and we ate a lot of jackrabbits."

Schafer Ranch — 1883
Lincoln County

Gary Schafer loads a bucket of cracked corn from a bin to feed early spring calves.

As the sun rises, Genevieve Eppich breaks hay bales to feed the sheep on her ranch near Mancos.

Tish Linke helps her family with branding chores by roping the calves and leading them to the fire.

SUMMER

Corpus A. Gallegos Ranch — Costilla County

While most of the immigrants to the Colorado Territory came from the east, a significant group of settlers came from the south, and their influence adds a rich heritage to our state.

When Mexico won independence from Spain in 1821, it resulted in improved trade between Mexico and the United States. The Mexican government thought it prudent, however, to extend its influence, and awarded land grants to citizens who would immediately settle the lands north of Santa Fe. The Sangre de Cristo Grant had excellent agricultural possibilities, and several attempts were made to settle the area, but Ute Indians drove away the would-be settlers. Finally, in the summer of 1851, seven men journeyed north from Taos and founded San Luis, Colorado's oldest town.

The men laid out the town as a typical Mexican village, with a plaza surrounded by adobe homes. This could double as a corral or as a stockade against raiding parties of Ute Indians. Just east of town land was set aside for a *vega*, a commons area where each resident was entitled to graze two horses, two burros, and two cows. The settlers dug irrigation ditches and planted gardens.

Dario Gallegos, one of the original settlers of San Luis, ran sheep and grew cauliflower, beets, and cabbage. The farm was called an *extencione* because it was divided into long strips along the river bottom, 500 feet wide by five miles long. Still a working ranch, the land remains in the family. Today the Gallegos hold the oldest water rights in the state, with decrees dated 1855 and 1856 confirming their rights to draw water from the San Antonio and Conejos rivers.

In 1857 Dario opened the first general store in town. His descendant, Felix Romero, now runs the store, the oldest continually operated family-owned business in Colorado — another centennial accomplishment!

A fierce devotion to the land was bred in the Gallegos family. Corpus Gallegos, grandson of Dario, remembers his father, Celestino, telling him, "Get an education, but never sell the land. You can always come back to it."

"The farm has given us most of our necessities," he continued. "I went to college, all my kids have gone to college." Corpus became a high school principal in Colorado Springs, but almost every weekend his family returned to San Luis to work on the ranch. "I remember those weekends," said Corpus' oldest son, Joe. "Because of them, I knew ranching was what I wanted to do."

The ranch remains in the family because of inventive and devoted practices. Family members have taken on other jobs as needed, but still work on the ranch. Joe received a degree in mechanical engineering from Colorado State University and spent four and a half years on oil rigs in the North Sea, Africa, and the Middle East. He'd work for 30 days on a rig, then return to San Luis with his paycheck. He would put the check and his time off into the ranch, and then put in another stint on the oil rigs.

During that time his younger brother, Jerry, took care of the ranch's daily operations. When Joe returned to ranching full time in 1985, Jerry then took the time to earn a degree, graduating in business from Western State College. Jerry now divides his time between the ranch and his work as a counselor with a job training program in Alamosa.

In addition to working outside jobs, the Gallegos family found it necessary to diversify. Their main product is beef cattle, having switched from sheep ranching in 1943. They continue to raise a few sheep as well as goats, geese, and horses, and they still harvest the orchard planted

Joe Gallegos and neighbor Prax Ortega discuss which cattle to send to market. Ortega is also a centennial rancher.

around the turn of the century. "It produces...when we don't have a freeze," said Corpus. "We get apples, cherries, and even apricots. A lot of canning goes on in town from that orchard."

In order to keep up with market trends, they have expanded into organic vegetables, growing crops such as English peas and Bolita beans. "There's a real demand for the Bolita bean, a little yellow bean similar to a pinto bean and very tasty," said Corpus. "We sell to markets in Denver and Santa Fe. Demand is high for organic foods."

Dedicated to reclaiming range land overgrazed by sheep in the early 1900s, Joe has planted native blue grama grass and western wheatgrass as well as two non-native varieties to replace unproductive sagebrush.

"A lot of neighbors treat their land as a commodity, something to make money off of," said Joe. "A farm is a treasure, not a commodity. We have fences that are over a hundred years old. The old folks put a lot here for us. You can't sell that."

At 8,000 feet, and receiving only nine inches of rain a year, the high desert farms and ranches of the San Luis Valley are made green by irrigation. The long narrow layout of the *extenciones* is particularly suited to ditch irrigation.

As majordomo, Joe is in charge of upkeep and water allocation for the San Luis People's Ditch, which is fed by mountain springs flowing into Culebra Creek. The local ranchers elect officers, collect dues, and maintain the waterway. Most of the work takes place in the spring, when the ditch must be cleaned of debris before the water starts running. In the old days, the water users did their own spring cleaning. Today, they hire someone.

Corpus is in charge of setting up the fields for irrigating and watering the crops. This has been his job since he was a little boy and he comes to the task naturally. "We've had people come out and survey the land to determine the most efficient way for the water to flow," Joe said, "but it never was as good as Dad getting down on his knees and deciding how to do it. He was born to it."

Once the crops are in, the fields will be flooded about every fourteen days, unless it rains. Wearing rubber boots and carrying a shovel, Corpus opens the headgates of the ditch. As the water gushes along the edges of the field, he deftly builds small earthen dams to guide the water along the rows of beans, making sure each row and each plant gets enough, but not too much, water. He starts in the early morning, tapering off before noon to avoid evaporation loss during the heat of the day. Work continues late in the afternoon past sunset, with the four acres of bolita beans watered by the end of the second day.

"I just love the smell of the soil getting wet for the first time in the spring," said Joe. "When the water hits the dry soil, it starts percolating and gurgling. When you listen to the water rushing along the rows, you think you can hear the plants say thank you."

Water is vital to the ranch and Joe works hard to protect it. To achieve that means lobbying against a nearby gold mine that uses cyanide in its leaching process, which, if spilled or accidently released into the water supply, could poison the ranch water. Although the mine provides local jobs, Joe wonders what the economic benefit will be to the community if the valley's water supply is ruined. Old-timers protected their water with guns. Today it's with vigilance and political savvy.

Corpus Gallegos takes a break as the sun sets on another day of irrigating fields in the San Luis Valley.

Gary Schafer prepares for a calf roping competition, a social event held once a week on his ranch near Boyero.

Schafer Ranch — Lincoln County

George Schafer was just eight years old when he became the man of the house. After his father died at the age of 40, George and his mother were left to run the homestead, a sheep ranch in Lincoln County. His father had worked the land for 15 years, creating a way of life that would endure for generations to come. The Schafer Ranch, like all centennial farms and ranches, survived because of steadfast determination.

Conrad Schafer had immigrated to the United States from Germany in 1870. Like many, he was drawn to the mountains of Colorado and the boom times of silver mining. After several years of working the mines near Central City, where he met and married Katherine, he had earned enough money to homestead.

By 1873 Conrad and Katherine had settled on 160 acres near the present-day town of Boyero. There they raised sheep, pasturing them on the windswept plains and watering them in Big Sandy Creek. Young George started helping with chores just as soon as he was big enough. When Conrad died in 1888, Katherine and George carried on with the help of friends and neighbors. As is the way in farming and ranching communities, neighbors pitched in whenever necessary, helping at lambing time or when the sheep needed to be sheared. George married the local schoolteacher in 1910. He and his wife, Zena, and their son, Bob, continued raising sheep until 1926, when a freak accident changed the ranch's course. Late one afternoon, a Schafer sheepherder fell asleep in the pasture while he was supposed to be watching the herd. The sheep wandered onto nearby railroad tracks and an oncoming freight train, unable to stop in time, killed nearly 100 sheep. George decided it was a good time to switch to cattle ranching.

The 1920s and '30s were hard times for ranchers. Land was going for as little as 50 cents an acre, and the price of sheep and cattle wasn't much more. Bob attended college with plans to return to the ranch after graduating, but the Great Depression interrupted his education. Bob quit college in 1928 to come home to help on the ranch where he was needed. A college friend came too, working for room and board and $25 a month.

Jobless men frequently hopped off passing trains, offering to work for food. They were hired as ranch hands, grateful for the work, something to eat, and a place to sleep. The Schafers soon bought a neighbor's land for back taxes, allowing them to expand the pasture for their cattle.

As the economy recovered, George helped found the First National Bank in Hugo and also served as Lincoln County Commissioner. Mother Nature, however, presented one challenge after another: a plague of grasshoppers devoured their grasslands in the late '30s. The Schafers fought back with insecticides, defeating the voracious insects, but the land suffered. Years later they experienced a drought so severe that they had to burn the thorns off of cactus so the cattle would have something to eat.

It takes a special commitment to ranch on the Colorado plains, where drought and grasshoppers and hail can be devastating. In winter, blizzards can rage for days on end with an intensity that requires a guide rope tied between the house and the barn so family members won't get lost.

Bob married his sweetheart, Erma Garlick, in 1936, and in the early '40s, sons Keith and Gary were born. Like many children in rural areas, the boys attended a one-room schoolhouse until the eighth grade and then attended public school in the town of Hugo.

Trying to develop more hardiness in his cattle, Bob brought Mexican brahma bulls into the herd, one of the first cattlemen in the area to try cross-breeding. (Years later, son Gary would be the first rancher to show longhorn steers at the National Western Stock Show in Denver.) He increased the size of the herd from 500 to 1,000, but soon realized that the land could not support that many cattle and that he would need to hire more hands. Bob quickly decided to reduce the size of the herd back to a manageable 500.

Bob took on other responsibilities. In 1958 he became president of the Colorado Cattleman's Association, and in 1960 he was elected to the Colorado House of Representatives, serving as a state congressman for twelve years. While Bob was in Denver being a politician, Gary learned ranch skills from the foreman and the ranch hands.

"They taught me the finer points — roping, building fences, doctoring cattle — and Dad taught me the business aspects of ranching," Gary recalled. "I had some good teachers while I was growing up, and I always knew I would come back to the ranch."

While work comes first, there's time for fun, too. A major community event every summer is the team-roping contest held once a week at the Schafer's. Friends and neighbors come from as far as forty miles away to compete in the contest, a sport that developed as an offshoot of daily ranch chores. "It started out in the pasture when you were doctoring cattle," explained Gary. "To get the animal down so you could do what was needed, one person would rope the head, another person the feet. I'm a 'header,' meaning I go for the head. It's the old-fashioned way, but it's the most humane, too, I think."

Some twenty-five ropers gather for practice sessions on Tuesday nights and on Thursdays they compete. Entry fees go into a pot from which prizes, such as belt buckles and saddles, will be bought. "On the Fourth of July we have team roping with a big barbecue, everyone bringing a potluck dish. Then in September, at the final event of the season, I give out the prizes," he continued. "We have a lot of fun."

Roping skills are honed in work, evident on an early Saturday in May when ten people show up at the Schafer Ranch to help brand calves. The herd is rounded up and corralled, the bawling calves separated from their mothers. Branding irons heat in a fire until the metal glows red. Two helpers, ropes in hand, slowly ride among the bawling, skittery calves. One by one they are roped and pulled over to the fire. Held down by two other helpers, each calf is then inoculated, castrated, branded, and returned to its mother.

The branding becomes an efficient assembly line operation, stopping just long enough so those working can switch chores. After three hot, dusty hours, they have branded and vaccinated more than 150 calves — just like Gary's dad did, just like his grandfather did. The rhythms of the seasons don't change on a ranch, and sometimes the methods don't either.

After the evening's team-roping competition, Gary Schafer's daughter, Kate, relaxes on Dad's lap.

Irrigation sprinklers, lifeblood of the Colorado plains,
water fields in large circular patterns on the Godsey Family Farm near Wray.

Eddie Linke cuts hay on the Cottonwood Ranch near Granby.

Ranch hands from the Hotchkiss Ranch move sheep to summer pasture on Kebler Pass.

I, who had wanted silk, a creamy lace
Orchids — and soft white fur about my face
I wanted the South Seas, I wanted fame
Desire, burned in my heart a steady flame.
But I have had the humble things instead.
The simple rites of "Just a cup of tea,
"A baby's smile, a lighted open door
A road that led you always back to me.

And if I'd known, just four and fifty years ago
this pathway, lighted by Love's steady glow
My hand in yours — I'd brush away the tears.
And start back with you, through the long,
long years.

Written by Florence Sponsel
for her husband, Frank
(parents of Genevieve Eppich)

Eppich Ranch—1887
La Plata County

Genevieve Eppich brings water to her son, Tom, while he takes a break from field work.

Ward Ranch, Saguache.

Derek Godsey waits for his father and brothers to arrive at the Yuma County Fair with their steers.

Jacob and Margaret Yount heard of the opportunities in Colorado from a former Virginia neighbor who had moved to the state. They followed his advice and brought their family to what is now Yuma County in 1888. Today the farm is owned by Jacob and Margaret's great granddaughter, Joyce Schepler, and her husband, Dorvin, who raise cattle, hay, sunflowers, and wheat with the help of their son, Kirk. The family has renovated a rock house built in 1890 and turned it into a museum, filling it with family diaries, furniture, and clothing from the homestead days. They open the museum for school classes or private groups.

Yount-Schepler Ranch — 1888
Yuma County

Wheat fields, Yount-Schepler Ranch.

After a fast-moving storm, workers on the Yount-Schepler Ranch near Vernon
check to see if the wheat is too wet to continue combining.

The Yount and Schepler families call it a day when rain prevents them from
harvesting wheat. "Damn that rain! Two more passes and we would have finished."

One of the Hotchkiss Ranch's dogs leads a flock being moved to summer pasture on Kebler Pass.

FALL

Ward Ranch — Saguache County

Women came west for the same reasons men did — for adventure, for love, for the prospect of wealth, or in hopes of improving their lot in life. Often these women left behind family and friends, never knowing if they would see them again. They lived on farms and ranches in isolation far from neighbors, bore children, and raised them with little or no medical assistance. It took a special character not only to survive these conditions, but also to surmount them.

One who did was Julia Ann Collins. Born on Wolf Island in the middle of the Saint Lawrence River, she and her family moved to Iowa, where Julia finished school, earned a teaching certificate, and applied for a job at a one-room schoolhouse. She was told she could have the job if she could control the school bully, who had run off the previous teacher — a man.

Julia was a small woman, less than a hundred pounds, while the boy was large and bulky. The aspiring teacher told the boy to choose a seat and sit in it. "Make me," he responded. Snatching up a heavy inkwell from her desk, Julia threw it at his chest with all her might, and when he staggered, she grabbed his legs so he fell to the floor. She landed on his chest, grabbed both his ears and bumped his head on the floor until he gave up. She got the job and a raise.

Perhaps it was this audacious show of determination that endeared her to Nathan Ward, a neighbor's son. Born in England in 1837, Nathan, his parents, six brothers, and infant sister boarded a small sailing ship for New Orleans in 1860. From there, they went up the Mississippi River and homesteaded in Iowa. Nathan helped clear and plant the land, but his world soon fell apart. "I'm sorry, young man, you have consumption. I advise you to go west and never return to Iowa," was the advice he received.

Many hopeful adventurers headed to western gold fields in the spring of 1861, and Nathan made a deal with a man who had two wagons with teams of oxen. Nathan drove one team, pulling a wagonload of supplies on a trip that took two and a half months. He slept on the ground at night, always careful to encircle his bedroll with a rope, for he'd been told rattlesnakes would not cross a horsehair rope. By the time he reached Colorado, his consumption was cured.

Nathan worked placer mines in Georgia Gulch near Breckenridge until September 1861, when he joined the First Colorado Cavalry to fight in the Civil War. Hunting game for the troops building Fort Garland, he surveyed the countryside near Blanca Peak. Through his spotting scope he spied a green valley with trees and a stream. The sight of that beautiful valley never left his mind.

Discharged from the army in 1864, Nathan worked for the Union Pacific Railroad and also on farms and ranches in the Denver area, where he met Jack Skelton, his future partner. Discussing the possibilities of ranching in Colorado, Jack mentioned that he knew where he could buy some horses, and Nathan replied, "And I know the place to raise them."

The two of them traveled to Saguache in 1869 and filed homestead claims on the very spot Nathan had seen through his spy glass five years earlier. They then purchased Texas longhorns and hired a man to tend them while they improved their homesteads, building barns and corrals. Nathan and his partner may not have known how to herd or even rope, but they learned to improvise when necessary.

When they needed a steer to slaughter for meat, Nathan and Jack would drive the animal into a nearby bog. After the longhorn was safely

---

Opposite: Larry Ward looks up from shoeing a horse during a cattle drive.

mired, they would shoot it, and then use oxen to pull the carcass out for butchering. "They sure weren't cowboys," Nathan's great-grandson, Larry Ward, chuckled as he related the tale.

It was during a visit to his parents in Iowa that Nathan became engaged to Julia Collins. She traveled to Denver and they were married in 1875. Their two-week "honeymoon" was spent on a lumber wagon returning to Saguache.

Nathan and Julia had three sons and one daughter, who died at the age of 15 when she was caught in a fierce winter blizzard. Julia seemed unable to overcome the grief of losing her beloved daughter, but the birth of Mildred, her first granddaughter, helped to ease the pain. Later, Julia assisted at the birth of her second granddaughter, and as she prepared to leave at the end of three months, she announced, "You have another girl now, so I am taking Mildred home with me."

The Ward Ranch was located near the Los Piños Indian agency, where the Utes received their government provisions. When supplies were distributed, as many as 70 tepees were set up in a clearing between Los Piños and Cochetopa creeks, about fifteen miles away.

Chief Ouray and his wife, Chipeta, stopped regularly to pick wild currants growing near the ranch. One time, Ouray brought two young grandsons for a visit just as Julia was taking fresh bread from the oven. She cut two slices, spread them with butter, and coated them with sugar. The boys quickly ate the bread, center first and then the crust.

Nathan's son, Alba, took over the ranch in 1902. Alba's two boys, George and Bruce, later ran the ranch. When George's son, Larry, returned to the ranch in 1957 after five years of military service, he knew it was time to modernize. He convinced his father of the need for machinery, but because his father preferred horses, the Wards continued to use them to cut hay until 1972. "Dad was amused whenever a tractor got stuck in soft ground and had to be pulled out by horses," said Larry. "He was strictly a horseman."

"Most everything I learned was from Dad and Granddad," he continued. His grandfather told him always to watch the beavers and the cattle for a sign of how severe the coming winter would be. "In 1972 beavers were building dams all summer on the creek, and the cattle were trying to come off summer pasture about the first of August, instead of October as usual. I figured we were in for a hard winter."

So Larry bought all the hay he could. He paid $35 a ton and his father thought he was "crazier than hell." By the first of December, they had three feet of snow, temperatures hovered around zero, and they didn't see the ground again until spring. By January everyone wanted to buy hay. Larry sold all he had stockpiled, making enough profit that he fed his own cattle for free that winter. "I never tried to gouge anybody on the price. I would ask them what it was worth, and it was usually worth a lot more than I paid for it," he said.

Today Larry splits ranch chores with his son, Rick. As summer turns to fall, they spend long days in the hay fields. After the hay is in, they start gathering cows from summer pasture, with their dependable cow dogs by their side. "When the cattle go into the willows, a dog's as good as three men, because if a man went in there after a cow, the cow would go after him," explained Larry.

Julia would approve of that kind of tenaciousness.

Larry Ward rests with his dog, Fudd, while herding cattle. "I've had some of
these momma cows for so long, I just open the gate and they know where to go."

Dustin Eppich takes a break from helping his father with the oat harvest.

Eppich Ranch — La Plata County

21 September, 1886

Dear Brother John,

You must come to America. The work in the mines near Telluride is hard. But Colorado is beautiful and there is good land for farming…

It was a convincing letter George Sponsel wrote to his brother, who lived in the Bavarian region of Germany. And it couldn't have come at a better time. John, a farm boy of 23, wanted to avoid required military service, and his sweetheart, Anna, had been promised by her parents to wed an older man — much against her wishes. The pair booked passage on a steamer to New York and came by train to Denver, marveling at the vast open spaces in this new country. They brought all of their belongings with them, including a feather bed.

The young couple spoke no English, and in Denver they transferred to a train they thought was going to Durango, but they ended up in Salida. A train conductor, who was also a German immigrant, helped them reach their destination. Their first stop in Durango was St. Columbus Catholic Church to be married.

John and Anna homesteaded in Thompson Park, between Hesperus and Mancos, where other Germans had already settled. The land had many pine trees, which they cut for a house and also sold to a local sawmill. Their first year in a strange land must have been frightening. Worse, it was so dry that Anna could only use a cup of water a day for her precious garden; it was small, but essential for food.

Despite the aridity, John thought the land would be good for growing oats. He was right. His oat crops were legendary, and he became known as the "Oat King." In 1917 the *Mancos Times-Tribune* reported that he harvested and threshed 16,000 bushels of oats with his own machinery, with all labor done by the family. John's philosophy was "big farm, big family, big yields."

John and Anna had 13 children, losing one to whooping cough and two in the 1919 flu epidemic. Their son Frank, born in 1889, started working on the ranch full time after only a few years of grade school. He married Florence in 1916, and they stayed on the ranch when John and Anna moved to a house they had built in Durango.

John still hitched his favorite mare, Babe, to the buggy for the trip from town to the ranch. One summer day, he and Babe were trotting through dry, dusty Lightner Creek when a neighbor passed in a car, choking them in a cloud of dust. John wrote a check for a Hudson Super-Six the next day.

John still clung to the old ways where the ranch was concerned though. When Frank bought the first tractor, a Farmall, in 1929, his father took one look and asked, "How is that little thing going to run the thresher?"

Frank and Florence's daughter, Genevieve, born in 1919 and one of four girls and five boys, still lives in her parent's house. She remembers the Depression as a particularly tough time; the children wore underwear made from flour sacks, and it was "make do" with what they had in every way.

"There wasn't any money. What little cash the folks had, they had to save to pay taxes. Everything else was trade," she said reflectively.

"One day we were at the blacksmith's shop and a farmer came by with a load of apples for sale. Dad said he didn't have any money, but could trade some oats. Even though he had a team of horses, the farmer said he didn't need any oats and drove away. You can't imagine how much we wanted an apple. All these years later I still remember how much we wanted those apples."

The entire family pitched in to do chores. At threshing time the neighbors came to help, and Florence and the girls would have to feed two meals a day to more than 20 people. "We loved it when we were finally old enough to help in the fields and were able to sit and eat with the men," Genevieve chuckled.

She married George Eppich in 1946, and they took over the ranch that year. They had three boys and five girls, but that didn't keep Genevieve in the house. She continued to help in all aspects of the ranch, driving a team of horses for field work, cutting and raking hay, and feeding stock. That experience was needed after George was killed in a tractor accident in 1971.

Soon after the funeral and before the family was over the shock of his death, a real estate man called on Genevieve, asking if she wanted to sell. "Many hours were spent with a baby on my lap while cutting hay with a team of horses. I look back and wonder how we did it, but we are still here. I was born in this house and I'll die here. No real estate guy's getting this away from me," she said firmly.

In those years she rose at 4:00 A.M., when the lights turned on in the chicken house to encourage the hens to lay eggs. She fed them and the sheep, milked two cows, and fixed breakfast before driving the school bus at 7:00 A.M., a job she held for 26 years. After delivering the children to school, she would come home and collect eggs from the 800 to 900 hens and, at three o'clock in the afternoon, go back to school to drive the children home.

Then came more chores. "After supper you had to wash the eggs and candle them to see if they were good," Genevieve continued. "I don't ever want another chicken, but I still like my sheep."

Genevieve raises Columbia sheep, prized for the length of their wool. The lambs are born about the middle of March, and this year she's expecting several sets of triplets. "Some of those poor ewes can hardly waddle along," she said sympathetically. Last year they produced four sets of triplets, and the year before, 14 sets.

Ten peacocks roam the yard. Her husband gave her the first one, and, in subsequent years, her children have given her more. The birds strut around, fanning iridescent tails in proud display, roosting on top of the barn or the house, and greeting the day or any strange movements with a piercing shriek that sounds like a child in distress. "You can just about tell if someone's around or if a storm is coming," she said comfortably.

Today, slowed by arthritis, Genevieve still milks a few cows and tends her prized sheep. Her son, Tom, and grandson, Dustin, live in another house on the land and take care of the oats and cattle. Tom works a job at King Coal in Hesperus, hoping that he can soon ranch full time without the burden of heavy debt.

During the fall, Tom and Dustin finish the harvesting and shred and store the oats. Around the first of October, depending on the weather, Tom will ride north on the ranch and start gathering cows from their summer pasture.

On a crisp October morning, when the leaves are falling and the chill is in the air, Genevieve still starts her morning by feeding the sheep. Her peacocks screech loudly, heralding a change in the weather. She puts in two hours of work before many people are awake.

"There's no way I could live in town. I like to work," she declares. "Tom's working really hard, too. He wants to hang on to the ranch. I'm glad someone wants to."

Tom Eppich and a neighbor herd cattle off summer pasture near Mancos.

Eddie, Trey, and Jolene Linke start out early to round up and load cattle for shipping.

Larry Ward tends to Meany after the dog was kicked while herding cows.

Dallas Godsey, retired, still helps his son Don during harvest time.

John Hotchkiss and a driver count sheep before loading them in a truck for market.

Brian Farmer helps load sheep for market on the Hotchkiss Ranch.

The log cabin to which Nathan Ward brought his bride, Julia Ann Collins of Iowa, in 1875, was tiny. It had no windows and the only light came down the chimney, built narrow so an Indian could not sneak down it. They lived there only two months before moving to a larger house, but Julia hated the honeymoon cabin so much that, in later years, she tried to burn it down. Fondly remembering the lush greenery of Iowa with its plenteous trees and verdant grasses, she had a hard time accepting the starkness of the Colorado high plains. "This country is fit only for men and mules," she would say, "but not for women."

Ward Ranch — 1874
Saguache County

Larry Ward with his three dingos — Meany, Runt, and Fudd.

Genevieve Eppich heads to the ranch house after feeding her sheep.

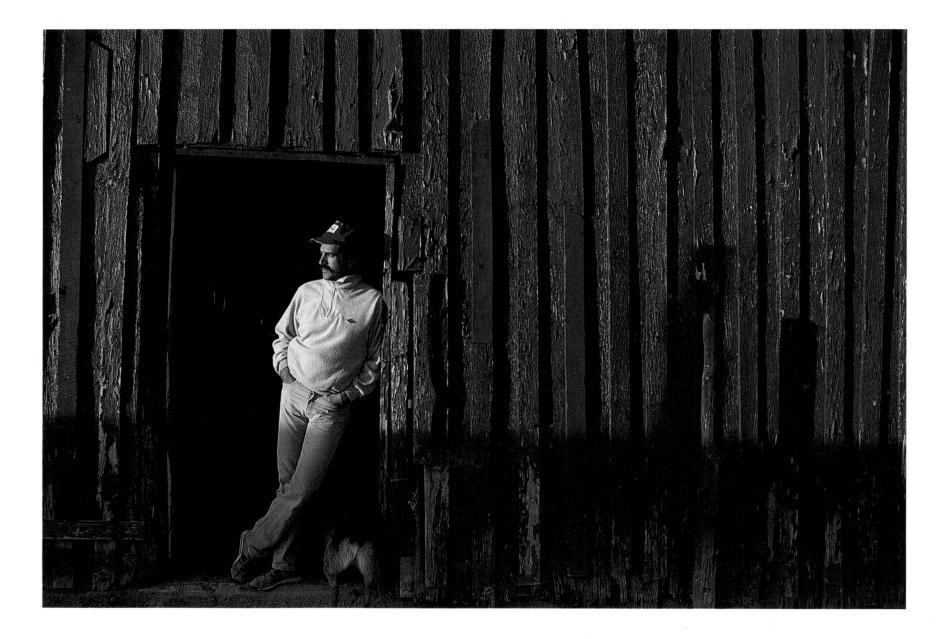

Joe Gallegos enjoys a sunset in the San Luis Valley.

A Gallegos ranch hand uses a bicycle as well as a cattle dog to move cows between pastures.

The Godseys work under a harvest moon to fix an auger that broke during the middle of corn harvest.

WINTER

Linke Ranch — Grand County

Skiing may seem an unlikely legacy on a ranch — but not in Colorado. A few days after Christmas in 1883, Emil Linke strapped on skis and headed across snowy meadows to fetch the midwife to help deliver the first of ten Linke children. Today, Emil's great-grandson, Trey, teaches skiing at Winter Park Ski Area and lives on the Middle Park Ranch, where he helps with chores.

Emil left his home near Leipzig, Germany, in 1866 at the age of twenty to come to America. He worked as a carpenter in West Virginia for eleven years before the magic of gold lured him west. He lived in Denver for five years, working as a carpenter, and then went to Leadville to pan for gold, but without success. Emil had better luck in Silverton, where he and a partner hit a vein of silver in what they called the Iowa Mine. Without the resources to develop the claim, they ended up selling it for $6,000.

Flush with success, Emil returned to Denver in 1882, bought a house, and spent time enjoying his new-found wealth. He frequented the German Turverein for schnapps and a little company, playing the zither and socializing. A young fraulein who worked in a German restaurant caught his eye; he and Sophie Weil were married in March 1883.

Feeling that Emil enjoyed dancing and schnapps a bit too much, Sophie encouraged him to return to the mountains and homestead before all the money was gone. They crossed Rollins Pass in a loaded covered wagon that summer and settled on Eight Mile Creek, a tributary of the Fraser River. Their homestead was in the wide and beautiful valley on a stagecoach route through Middle Park.

Emil cut trees to build a log cabin, a barn, and corrals. He cleared sagebrush for pastures and surveyed and trenched irrigation ditches.

All supplies for the family came by wagon twice a year from Georgetown. The children were always baffled as to why there was such mystery about the fall shipment, not realizing their Christmas presents were included.

German was spoken around the house and the children didn't learn English until they were school age. By the early 1900s there were six children in need of an education and the nearest school was in Hot Sulphur Springs, eight miles away. Emil built a one-room log building, called it a schoolhouse, and hired a teacher from Denver to live with and teach the children.

Emil died in 1917, leaving serious financial problems. Around the turn of the century, he had taken mortgages on land already paid off to purchase more property — several parcels adjacent to the homestead and a speculative purchase in Utah. A poor economy made it difficult to make payments, and the entire family worked to refinance the loans and avoid foreclosure.

Son Edwin took over the homeplace in 1926 after "proving up" on a 360-acre homestead of his own. Four years later he married Susie Winifred, a preacher's daughter from Texas, who had come to the ranch to teach his younger brothers and sisters. She wrote she was "entranced with the breath-taking views from my room. Little did I dream this would become my permanent home."

Edwin and Susie entered married life at the same time the country was entering the Great Depression. They had payments on 3,000 acres of mortgaged land and some 1,200 head of sheep and cattle to feed. In the drought of 1934 the well went dry, and a spring was their only source of water. Later that summer the hay meadow caught fire and burned, leaving them without hay for the following winter. Their only son, Eddie, about four at the time, remembers men from the Works Progress

Opposite: Eddie Linke breaks a hole in the ice to water his draft horses.

Administration building a barn and outbuildings on the ranch. The laborers were paid $1 a day, carpenters $2.

"One of my strongest memories from that time was government men coming to the ranch and killing most of our sheep," Eddie recalled. "They cut their throats, piled them in trucks, and drove off. Of course my father was paid by the government, which was trying to reduce the number of surplus sheep in the country. I don't know what they did with the slaughtered sheep." At that time sheep were only bringing about $2 a head, compared to $10 in 1919.

The Linkes survived the Depression without major tragedies, only to have one strike in the early 1940s when they were just beginning to prosper. On a cold, windy Sunday in February of 1942, Ed and a ranch hand were feeding sheep and cattle in a pasture a few miles from the house. Susie and the two children were attending a morning church service when a church elder whispered to her, "Your house is on fire."

Susie and the kids raced home to find flames shooting from the upstairs windows. They had added on to the original cabin Emil had built and, now, gusting winds and exploding oil tanks turned the house into an inferno. The Granby Fire Department could only save the barn and the outbuildings. By the time Ed arrived on horseback, all he could do was comfort his wife and children, watching helplessly as their possessions burned. Neighbors took them in and helped them rebuild, but family photographs, antiques, and other sentimental possessions could never be replaced.

Today Eddie runs the operation, now called the Cottonwood Ranch, where he raises cattle, quarter horses, and hay. Like his father, Eddie also married a schoolteacher. Lorraine taught school for 27 years in addition to helping with ranch chores and raising six children. The children are grown with lives of their own now, but they all return to help on the ranch when needed. Eddie works the ranch daily.

Just as his father and his grandfather did, Eddie uses a sled and a team of Belgian draft horses to feed hay to the cattle in winter. "I still use teams because they're cheaper and I can do the work myself," Eddie explained. "And some mornings, when it's too cold, a tractor won't start." When something's worked for a hundred years, there's not much reason to change.

On winter mornings, Eddie heads to the corral accompanied by Chili, a Dingo who would rather chase a stick than herd a cow. It's cold, below zero, and hoar frost has turned the metal gates into a grid of sparkling crystal. Sundance and Billy nicker softly as Eddie arrives. He talks gently to the horses while harnessing them. Then he leads them from the barn and hitches them to the heavy wood sled, piled high with hay.

First Eddie feeds the bulls in the pasture by the barn. Then the horses pull the sled slowly up a hill, their heavy breathing, the jingling of the harnesses, and the squeaking of the sled's runners on the snow the only sounds heard in the white pasture. Snow explodes from the horses' hoofs and sprays in Eddie's face as they gallop downhill past the quarter horses, shaggy with their winter coats. Then the Belgians slow to a stately pace as Eddie loosely secures the reins. He pushes hay off the wagon with a pitchfork as the sled passes the fields where the cows are wintering.

Using a homemade motorized hayfork, Eddie loads and transports three loads of hay before heading back to the house. On the steep hill out of the valley, he stops the sled to let the horses rest. Even in the cold, their coats glisten with sweat and steam rises from their backs. Turned loose in the corral, Sundance and Billy are rewarded with hay and a long drink of water. The next day they'll do it all over again.

Eddie Linke heads for the warmth of the house after feeding the cattle on a snowy winter day.

*The draft horses that pulled
the covered wagon from Iowa to
Yuma County, Colorado, would
be used to plow the virgin prairie
when W. Scott Godsey and his family
found a homestead site. To save the
horses' strength for that vital task,
Scott, his wife, Gertrude, and their
three small children walked most of
the way so they wouldn't add more
weight to the wagon. Walking
through shoulder-high prairie grass
for weeks on end, they stayed behind
the wagon to avoid unseen rattlesnakes.
They arrived in April of 1887.
Son Lynn was born in May.*

Godsey Family Farm — 1887
Yuma County

Don and Chad Godsey straighten feed bunks before feeding the cattle.

Godsey Family Farm — Yuma County

Water — too much or too little — is a constant thread in the Godsey family saga. W. Scott Godsey left an Iowa farm with fertile soil because it was too often under water, flooded year after year by the rising Missouri River. In 1887 Scott and his family headed west, looking for land to settle.

They homesteaded twelve miles southwest of Wray, Colorado, between Chief Creek and the Republican River. Water was available and didn't threaten to wash them out. Scott's wife, Gertrude, whom he had married in 1880, was an adventurous woman, having left New York to teach in Illinois and then Iowa. Gertrude, Scott, and their four young children lived in a dugout covered with the canvas top from their wagon until a sod house could be built.

Several years of drought and poor economy during the early 1890s led the family to join a wagon train bound for Buena Vista, Colorado. Scott worked in the copper mines, earning enough money to feed his family through the winter of 1892-93. They returned to their homestead that spring, staying long enough to "prove up" their claim, then went back to Iowa to wait for better times. In 1899 the Godsey family returned to Colorado for good.

Range cattle and the elements had all but destroyed their sod house, so they rented a shack from a neighbor while building the five-room frame house they would eventually call home. Scott purchased a thresher and made extra money working for neighbors. Things were going well, and the family was growing; Scott and Gertrude had eleven children, although four died very young.

Scott returned to Iowa once more to bring back a small herd of cattle, walking some 350 miles each way. Buffeted by rain, sleet, and snow, Scott was cold and wet for most of the trip. The journey would take a serious toll on his health, and he died in 1908.

In 1910 Gertrude took over an adjacent homestead that had been relinquished by the previous owner. When he came of age, her oldest son bought another neighboring property. All of these parcels made up the Godsey Family Farm, where they ran beef cattle and raised dryland crops. Donald Dee, the youngest, farmed the homeplace, and when his son, Dallas, returned from World War II in 1945, the two established a dairy farm.

Dallas' family moved into the large homestead house in 1966. His wife, Mildred, taught school while Dallas ran the dairy operation and raised cattle, hogs, and milo, a drought-resistant grain. A heart attack in 1974 meant Dallas had to close down the dairy operation. Daughter Berna returned from Peace Corps service in the Philippines to help, and in 1977 son Don, who had been teaching vocational agriculture school in Greeley, moved to the farm with his wife, Debbie. "I always wanted to come back to the farm, and that seemed like the time," said Don.

He tried a new kind of agriculture. Great irrigating sprinklers, tapping deep into the Ogallala Aquifer far below the prairies, were installed, and the whole family pitched in to remove fences so the sprinklers could revolve unimpeded in huge circles. The benefits of dependable water have been dramatic: in the Dust Bowl year of 1934, the Godseys harvested only 500 bushels of corn from 300 acres; today, with circle irrigation, they harvest approximately 60,000 bushels from that same 300 acres.

"Our three center-pivot sprinklers each have an arm about 1,200 feet in length, which takes about two-and-a-half days to complete a circle,"

Don explained. "We put about an inch to an inch and a quarter of water on an area. Each sprinkler covers 160 acres, while our big pivot, about 1,980 feet long, covers 320 acres. We usually start in late June, and run them all day, five days a week, through July and August. The corn is planted the first of May, and we harvest at the end of October or early November, according to the weather.

"The next generation might not have this particular kind of irrigation," Don continued. "Hopefully, with all the technology, they'll find ways to use water more efficiently."

Water and weather. These are make-it or break-it factors on farms and ranches, and the Godseys, in addition to growing corn, also raise cattle.

On a cold March day in 1993, the weather was creating problems for Don, who had newborn calves to tend. A storm had blown across eastern Colorado the night before, leaving six inches of snow and 30-mile-per-hour winds. It was deadly weather for a newborn calf.

As the sun dropped closer to the horizon, the wind made the fields bitter cold. Don and his hired man, Steve, had been with a mother cow that needed special attention, and it had been a few hours since the other cows, scattered across several snowy corn fields, had been checked.

"Sometimes cows aren't good mothers, especially first-calf heifers," Don explained. "If they fail to clean their calf and don't get it to nurse, the calf won't last long in this weather." Debbie, Don's wife, had warmed up two calves in an equipment shed. Now that son, Chad, was home from school, the family split off in three pickup trucks, driving through corn fields, ready to give lessons in motherhood.

Don reunited a cow with her calf after the mom had wandered off. Back in the truck, Steve's voice came over the two-way radio. "I've got one that's barely breathing. If I don't get him warmed up, we're going to lose him." Chad and Steve raced back to the machine shed and placed the calf in a tub of warm water and began massaging its heart, their only chance of reviving the cold, hungry calf that had spent its first hour of life lying alone on a snow-covered field where the howling winds dropped temperatures to -35 degrees. Steve's voice came back on the radio: "Don, he didn't make it. Guess we didn't get to him soon enough."

The wind continued to howl and the sun and temperature to fall. The headlights of the truck shone on a cow licking a dead calf — dead not from neglect, but it probably just wasn't strong enough from the start. It would be a long night of driving the fields, watching for cold calves.

Later, as the cloudless sky turned from orange to deep blue to purple then black, the Godseys got the break they needed: the wind died. Although the temperature was -5 degrees, the wind chill was no longer a danger and lessened the fear of losing more calves during the night. All the Godseys lost was sleep.

Unexpected weather is the norm for farmers and ranchers. "We just try to do things the best we can, to see if we can keep our farm the same, or better, for the future," said Don, looking back at his great-grandfather's legacy.

The Godsey's oldest son marries his high school sweetheart.
Younger brother Derek's hair needed a little fixing for the family portrait.

*"The Dutchman will soon
be froze out, dried out,
or starved out," predicted a
neighbor who watched Emil Linke
struggle to establish a homestead
in 1883. Only a few years a later,
that same neighbor would have to
buy hay from the successful rancher,
and more than a hundred
years later, Emil's descendants
still grow hay on their Middle Park
Ranch, where they raise cattle
and quarter horses.*

Linke Ranch — 1883
Grand County

**Eddie Linke maneuvers a wagon piled with hay
through snowy pastures to feed his cattle.**

Winter temperatures of minus 15 degrees, Cottonwood Ranch.

Gary Schafer picks up mail at the "post office" in Boyero.

Following afternoon chores, Genevieve Eppich stops for a moment in the warmth of the sun.

Larry Ward fixes a piece of equipment for his hay baler. The long months of winter are a time for repairs.

Gary Schafer eyes the sky on his ranch near Boyero. "Any rain we get out this way is a blessing and we sure could use some now."

COLORADO CENTENNIAL FARMS & RANCHES

As of August 1993

ADAMS COUNTY
Windler Homestead, 1881

ALAMOSA COUNTY
Maddux Brothers, 1874
Jones Ranch, 1884

ARCHULETA COUNTY
Archuletta Ranch, 1876
Farrow Ranch, 1879
Macht Ranch, Inc., 1883

BACA COUNTY
Crill Ranch, 1884
McEndree Ranch, 1883
Ward Family Farms, 1889

BENT COUNTY
Marlman Farm, 1888
McClave Ranch, Inc., 1892

BOULDER COUNTY
Dodd Farm, 1884
Ewing Farm, 1893
Faivre Ranch, 1881
Moll Bauernhof Farm, 1881
Hycrest Farm, 1876
John Aken Laughlin Farm, 1885
Leyner Farm, 1864
Madison Farm, 1890
Mayhoffer Farm, 1870
McCaslin Farm, 1877
Montgomery Farm, 1880
Montgomery Homestead, 1883
Seal-Scates Homestead, 1885
Steele's Flying Triangle, 1870
The Chuck Waneka Farm, 1883
Zweck Farm, 1866

CHAFFEE COUNTY
Hutchinson Ranch, 1867

CLEAR CREEK COUNTY
Guanella Ranch, 1860

CONEJOS COUNTY
Gonzales Farm, 1870
Stewart Ranch, 1863

COSTILLA COUNTY
Corpus A. Gallegos Ranches, 1860
A. Prax Ortega Farm, 1851
Rio Culebra Ranch, 1863

CROWLEY COUNTY
Roland Dean Rusher Ranch, 1870

CUSTER COUNTY
Brandenburg Ranch, 1879
Elton Camper Ranch, 1874
Frank Kennicott Ranch, 1870
Koch Ranch, 1871
San Isabel Ranch, 1872

DELTA COUNTY
Mt. Lamborn Ranches, Ltd., 1889
Jones Polled Herefords, 1886
River Road Ranch, 1885

DELTA & GUNNISON COUNTY
Hotchkiss Ranches, Inc., 1881

DOLORES COUNTY
Knight/Bankston Ranch, 1879

DOUGLAS COUNTY
Eagle Mountain Ranch, 1890
Feather Ridge Farm, 1891
The Kelty's Bar Mill Iron Ranch, 1873
Rock Ridge, 1886
Woodhouse Ranch, 1873

EAGLE COUNTY
Calhoun's Lazy Ranch, 1886
Slaughter Ranch, 1892

EL PASO COUNTY
Green Valley Ranch, 1878

EL PASO & ELBERT COUNTY
B/K Ranch, 1891

ELBERT COUNTY
Anderson Ranch, 1888
Beuck Land Company Ranch, 1874
Carnahan Ranches, Inc., 1860
Keyhole Hereford Ranch, 1869
The Carl Maul Ranch, 1880

FREMONT COUNTY
Green Ranch, 1868
Griffin Ranch, 1870

GILPIN COUNTY
Rudolph Ranch, 1878

GRAND COUNTY
Linke Ranch, 1883
MY Ranch (E.C. Yust Homestead), 1884
Sheriff Ranch, 1881

GUNNISON COUNTY
Ralph R. Allen & Sons, Inc., 1890
Flick Ranch of Quartz, 1881
Vevarelle Esty Ranch, 1884

HUERFANO COUNTY
Goemmer Land & Livestock Co., 1876
Mildred Pino Shafter Ranch, 1889
Ritter Ranch, 1888
Woodring Family Ranch, 1893

HUERFANO AND PUEBLO COUNTIES
Butler Ranch, 1882

JACKSON COUNTY
Fred Brands & Son, 1892
Kohlman Ranch, 1879
North Park Registered Herefords, 1887
Wattenberg Ranch, Inc., 1884

JEFFERSON COUNTY
Baughman Family, 1886
Church Ranch, 1869
Rooney Ranch, 1859
The Wise Ranch/Wise Homestead, 1870

LAKE COUNTY
Smith Ranch, 1881

LA PLATA COUNTY
Eppich Ranch, 1887
The Frank Wommer Ranch, 1878
Ed Wommer Ranch, 1883

LARIMER COUNTY
Peep O'Day Park, 1878
Osborn Ranch, 1861
Roberts Cattle Co., 1873
The Willis Farm, 1877

LAS ANIMAS COUNTY
Duran Farm, 1889
Vigil-Gallino Ranch, 1888
Jose Urbano Vigil Ranch, 1869

LINCOLN COUNTY
Schafer Ranch, 1873

LOGAN COUNTY
Bar Three Ranch, 1876
Knudsen Farm, 1885
Peter Lantz Farm, 1889
Lazy 3N Ranch, 1890
Livestock Brand: H, 1889
Rieke Pasture, 1887
A.H. Tetsell Farm & Ranch, 1885

MESA COUNTY
ZF Ranch, 1885

MINERAL COUNTY
Soward Ranch, 1886

MOFFAT COUNTY
Mack Family Ranch, 1883

MONTEZUMA COUNTY
Ritter-Schlegel-Lee Ranch, 1874

MONTROSE COUNTY
Jutten Ranch, 1883

MORGAN COUNTY
The Elms Farm, 1885
George W. Warner Farm, 1881

OTERO COUNTY
Round Ranch, 1890
Carlyle R. Todd Horse Farm, 1888

OURAY COUNTY
Fournier's Ranch, 1890
Humphrey Ranch, 1887
Long Pine Ranch, 1891
Smith Brothers Ranch, 1886

PARK COUNTY
Estabrook Park Ranch, 1874
The Deer Valley Park Association, 1883
The Salt Works Ranch, 1862

PHILLIPS COUNTY
Frank Bjorklun Farm, 1888
Ewegan Farm, 1887
Hargreaves Farm & Ranch, 1885
Johnston Ranch, 1888
McGuire Farms, 1886
The Unzicker Homestead, 1891

PROWERS COUNTY
Donald C. McMillin Farm, 1876
R. M. McMillin Ranch, 1876

PUEBLO COUNTY
Cawlfield Farms, 1891
San Carlos Ranch, 1889

RIO BLANCO COUNTY
Anderson Ranch, 1886
Burke Brothers, 1887
Hauck Ranch, 1887
David Smith Ranches, Inc., 1892
Warren, Rector, Keele Farm, 1888

RIO GRANDE COUNTY
Elkhorn Ranch, 1886
Fuchs Ranches, Inc., 1880
Curtis W. & Lora Jean Nelson Ranch, 1888
Off 'Island' Ranch, 1872
Dolores and Harvey Stephens Farm, 1871

ROUTT COUNTY
The Summer Ranch, 1889

SAGUACHE COUNTY
Russell's N Lazy R Ranch, 1874
Ward Ranches, 1874

SEDGWICK COUNTY
J.A. Dawson Farm, 1887
Woodhams-Fourth Generation Farm, 1887

WASHINGTON COUNTY
Deering Farm, 1887
Diamond Farms, 1893

WELD COUNTY
Clark-Rudolph Farm, 1889
Conlin-Craven Farm, 1888
Craven-Shable Farm, 1890
Daniels' Homestead, 1872
Dale Ewing Farm, 1864
Emerson Farms, Inc., 1892
Epple Ranch, 1890
5 M Farm Company, Inc., 1891
Gerry Farm, 1871
Gray Farm, 1885
Ivan & Joan Grein Farm, 1892
Grommon Ranch, 1876
Gustafson Farm, 1889
Gustafson Farm, 1892
Leis-Abbett Ranch, 1875
Loloff Farms Inc., 1889
William Story McElroy Farm, 1871
Roland Miller Farm, 1880
Milne Farm, 1888
Wes Moser and Sons, Inc., 1890
Park Farm & Feedlot, 1888
The Riggs Farm, 1889
Smillie-King-Severin Farm, 1891
Southard Farm, 1878
Wadlin-Goetzel Farms, 1870
White-Plumb Farm, 1881

YUMA COUNTY
George L. Akey Farm, 1886
Blachburg Ranch, 1887
Bradford Ranch, 1888
Busby Farm, 1888
Fleer Ranch, 1886
Godsey Family Farm, 1887
Greene/Hill Farm, 1887
Helling Farm, 1887
Idler Farm, 1887
KW-Korf Homestead, 1886
Lengel Ranch, 1886
C. Henry Moellenberg Farm, 1887
National Homestead, 1887
Pfeiler Farm, 1886
The S Lazy Ranch, 1886
Shaw Ranch, 1887
Wingfield Farm & Ranch, 1886
Dean & Barbara Witte Farm, 1892
Yount-Schepler Ranch, 1888

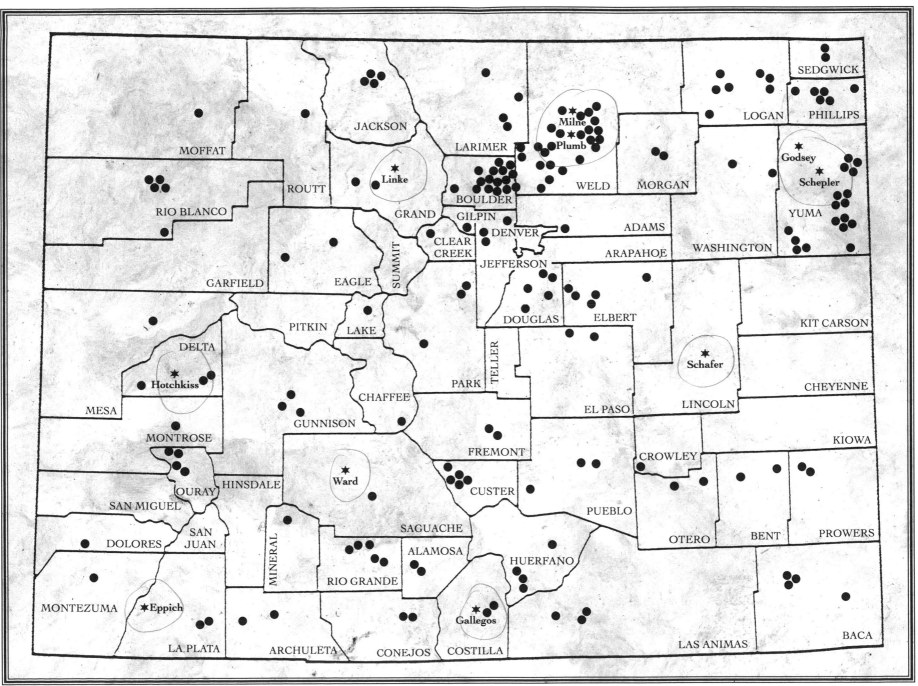

SEDGWICK

LOGAN

PHILLIPS

MOFFAT

JACKSON

LARIMER

Milne

Plumb

WELD

MORGAN

Godsey

Schepler

YUMA

ROUTT

Linke

RIO BLANCO

GRAND

BOULDER

GILPIN

DENVER

ADAMS

CLEAR CREEK

ARAPAHOE

WASHINGTON

GARFIELD

EAGLE

SUMMIT

JEFFERSON

DOUGLAS

ELBERT

KIT CARSON

PITKIN

LAKE

DELTA

TELLER

Schafer

CHEYENNE

MESA

Hotchkiss

PARK

CHAFFEE

EL PASO

LINCOLN

KIOWA

MONTROSE

GUNNISON

FREMONT

CROWLEY

OURAY

HINSDALE

Ward

CUSTER

PUEBLO

SAN MIGUEL

PUEBLO

OTERO

BENT

PROWERS

DOLORES

SAN JUAN

MINERAL

SAGUACHE

ALAMOSA

HUERFANO

MONTEZUMA

Eppich

RIO GRANDE

Gallegos

LAS ANIMAS

BACA

LA PLATA

ARCHULETA

CONEJOS

COSTILLA

● **Colorado Centennial Farms & Ranches**   ★ **Centennial Families Featured In This Book**